SECRETS OF THE ANIMAL WORLD

DINOSAURS
Monster Reptiles of a Bygone Era

MAR   2001

by Eulalia García
Illustrated by Gabriel Casadevall and Ali Garousi

Gareth Stevens Publishing
MILWAUKEE

For a free color catalog describing Gareth Stevens' list of high-quality books and multimedia programs, call 1-800-542-2595 (USA) or 1-800-461-9120 (Canada). Gareth Stevens Publishing's Fax: (414) 225-0377. See our catalog, too, on the World Wide Web: http://gsinc.com

The editor would like to extend special thanks to Richard Sajdak, Aquarium and Reptile Curator, Milwaukee County Zoo, Milwaukee, Wisconsin, for his kind and professional help with the information in this book.

Library of Congress Cataloging-in-Publication Data

García, Eulalia.
   [Dinosaurio. English]
   Dinosaurs: monster reptiles of a bygone era / by Eulalia García; illustrated by Gabriel Casadevall and Ali Garousi.
     p. cm. – (Secrets of the animal world)
   Includes bibliographical references and index.
   Summary: Describes the physical traits, social patterns, mating habits, and other characteristics of these fascinating reptiles.
   ISBN 0-8368-1497-5 (lib. bdg.)
   1. Dinosaurs–Juvenile literature. [1. Dinosaurs.] I. Casadevall, Gabriel, ill.
II. Garousi, Ali, ill. III. Title. IV. Series.
QE862.D5G2813 1996
567.9'1–dc20
                                           95-53865

This North American edition first published in 1996 by
Gareth Stevens Publishing
1555 North RiverCenter Drive, Suite 201
Milwaukee, Wisconsin 53212 USA

This U.S. edition © 1996 by Gareth Stevens, Inc. Created with original © 1993 Ediciones Este, S.A., Barcelona, Spain. Additional end matter © 1996 by Gareth Stevens, Inc.

Series editor: Patricia Lantier-Sampon
Editorial assistants: Jamie Daniel, Diane Laska, Rita Reitci

Printed in the United States of America

1 2 3 4 5 6 7 8 9 9 99 98 97 96

CONTENTS

THE WORLD OF THE DINOSAURS

Where dinosaurs lived

The dinosaurs were a group of land reptiles that dominated Earth long before humans. When dinosaurs first appeared 230 million years ago, Earth's continents were joined together in one mass, called Pangea. The dinosaurs could roam Earth without having to cross the open sea. To study dinosaurs today, paleontologists rely only on fossils. These fossils usually consist of bones or teeth — parts that decay slowly. Besides bones, footprint fossils have also been found, as well as fossils of dinosaur droppings that help show what the animals ate. The first clue to the dinosaurs' existence was the discovery of a tooth so large it could not possibly have belonged to any of today's creatures. Because of its similarity to the teeth of modern reptiles, scientists decided it must belong to an ancient and very large reptile.

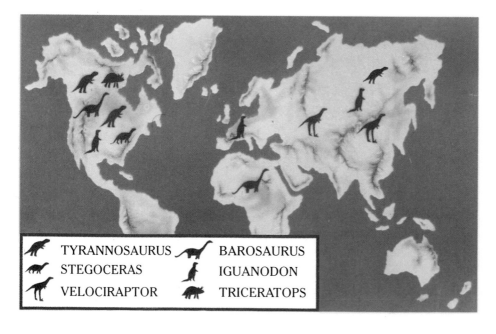

TYRANNOSAURUS	BAROSAURUS
STEGOCERAS	IGUANODON
VELOCIRAPTOR	TRICERATOPS

This map shows where some dinosaurs lived. The continents were not always separated as they are now, and not all dinosaurs lived at the same time.

DINOSAUR   LIZARD

The dinosaur's legs were better positioned for running because they came straight down from its body.

Neither lizard nor terrible

The word *dinosaur* means "terrible lizard," but these animals were not lizards, and they weren't so terrible. As reptiles, however, they did have scaly skin, and they laid eggs. Many of the largest dinosaurs were peaceful plant-eaters, or herbivores. Some of them weighed as much as 88 tons (80 metric tons), the same as twelve African elephants. The largest carnivore ever to walk on Earth was the terrible Tyrannosaurus rex, whose name means "king of the tyrant lizards." Like all meat-eating dinosaurs, it had long, sharp teeth that it used to tear the flesh from victims.

Tyrannosaurus rex's victims rarely escaped death. Its long, sharp, curving teeth allowed few escapes.

A handful of dinosaurs

Ninety million years ago, packs of carnivorous dinosaurs of the same species probably attacked herbivorous dinosaurs. The carnivores were feared hunters with terrible, sharp claws. One was the deadly Velociraptor ("swift predator"), whose remains were found with its claws still stuck in the belly of another dinosaur. Even more impressive in size and appearance was ferocious, meat-eating Tyrannosaurus rex.

Scientists only know about 1 percent of all the dinosaurs that ever lived.

STEGOSAURUS
(HERBIVORE)

APATOSAURUS/
BRONTOSAURUS
(HERBIVORE)

VELOCIRAPTOR
(CARNIVORE)

ANKYLOSAURUS
(HERBIVORE)

TOROSAURUS
(HERBIVORE)

TYRANNOSAURUS
(CARNIVORE)

Apatosaurus was an enormous herbivore that measured about 70 feet (21 meters), including its long neck and tail. Stegosaurus, an armor-plated dinosaur, was easily identified by the double row of plates down its back and the four spikes on the end of its tail, which it used to stab enemies. Ankylosaurus, another armor-plated dinosaur, had bony plates and spikes on its back and a bony club on the end of its tail. Torosaurus was a horned dinosaur, recognizable by its enormous bony collar.

INSIDE TYRANNOSAURUS REX

The most powerful meat-eating dinosaur was Tyrannosaurus rex. It was longer than eight adult humans laid end to end, taller than a giraffe, and heavier than an adult African elephant. It had a huge head, a long tail, and two tiny arms. Its internal organs may have looked similar to this illustration.

HIP
Dinosaurs can be classified according to the position of the hip bones. Tyrannosaurus, for example, had a "reptile-type" hip, and Triceratops had a "bird-type" hip.

SCALY SKIN
Dinosaurs had scaly skin, the same as reptiles today.

TAIL
A muscular tail helped T. rex keep its balance while running or attacking prey. By using its tail for balance, it could stand upright on two feet while attacking.

TAIL VERTEBRAE

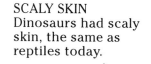

LEGS
Tyrannosaurus rex could run up to 18 miles (30 km) an hour. Because of its 8.8 tons (8 metric tons) of weight, it could only keep this speed up for a short distance.

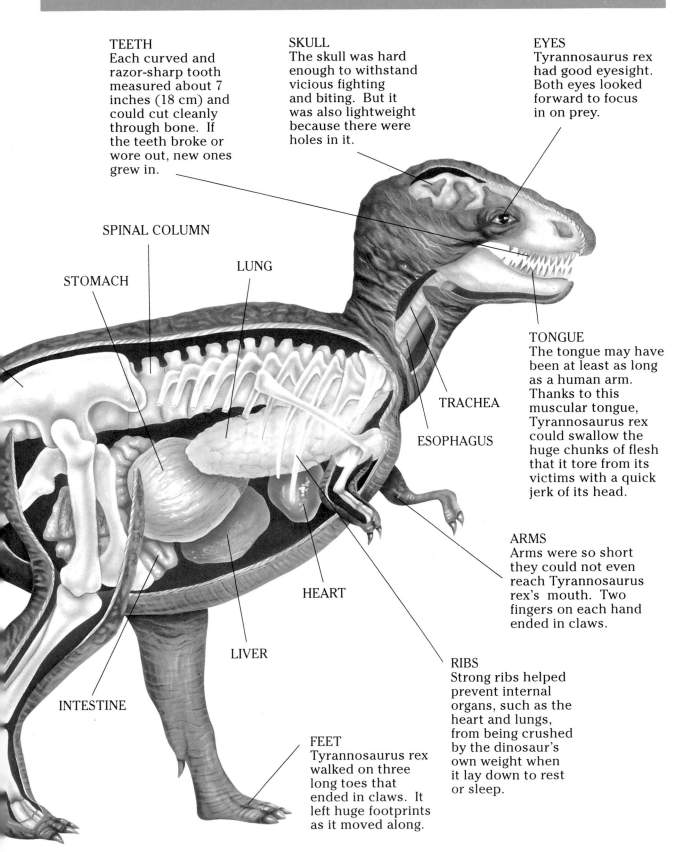

TEETH
Each curved and razor-sharp tooth measured about 7 inches (18 cm) and could cut cleanly through bone. If the teeth broke or wore out, new ones grew in.

SKULL
The skull was hard enough to withstand vicious fighting and biting. But it was also lightweight because there were holes in it.

EYES
Tyrannosaurus rex had good eyesight. Both eyes looked forward to focus in on prey.

SPINAL COLUMN

LUNG

STOMACH

TONGUE
The tongue may have been at least as long as a human arm. Thanks to this muscular tongue, Tyrannosaurus rex could swallow the huge chunks of flesh that it tore from its victims with a quick jerk of its head.

TRACHEA

ESOPHAGUS

ARMS
Arms were so short they could not even reach Tyrannosaurus rex's mouth. Two fingers on each hand ended in claws.

HEART

LIVER

RIBS
Strong ribs helped prevent internal organs, such as the heart and lungs, from being crushed by the dinosaur's own weight when it lay down to rest or sleep.

INTESTINE

FEET
Tyrannosaurus rex walked on three long toes that ended in claws. It left huge footprints as it moved along.

9

DINOSAURS RULE!

Power and might

Dinosaurs ruled Earth for 165 million years. Mammals first appeared during the time of the dinosaurs, and have ruled only for the 65 million years since the dinosaurs disappeared. Why were dinosaurs so successful? They were neither lacking in intelligence nor clumsy, as scientists once thought they were. In fact, many dinosaurs were bipeds that could run swiftly to follow prey or escape from predators. The most ferocious meat-eating dinosaurs,

If dinosaurs had walked with their legs coming out the sides of their bodies like other reptiles, they would have left huge furrows in the ground.

such as Deinonychus, moved on two feet. These terrifying predators probably hunted large prey in packs. Several Deinonychus would ambush a giant herbivore, which would eventually die of exhaustion and loss of blood.

Bloodthirsty Deinonychus may have hunted in packs.

that some dinosaurs were the size of hens?

Dinosaurs were the largest land creatures that ever lived, but not all of them were enormous. Hen-sized Compsognathus, for example, weighed only about 9 pounds (4 kilograms) and was 24 inches (60 cm) long. It was probably a fast runner because of its light but strong back legs, and its long tail was used for balance. Compsognathus was a clever, active predator that ate insects and small vertebrates. Mussaurus was an even smaller dinosaur; it was the size of a blackbird and, like Compsognathus, was an agile runner.

A hungry tyrant

Its imposing appearance, terrifying roar, and insatiable appetite made Tyrannosaurus a feared predator. Few animals would have dared attack it. Tyrannosaurus stalked its prey by sight, smell, and sound. At the same time, it watched for competitors that might approach. It would leap on its prey with a mighty roar before sinking its teeth in. Tyrannosaurus used its claws to hold the victim down, while it pulled off the flesh in chunks with its razor-sharp teeth.

Tyrannosaurus's short arms were probably not much help in catching and holding prey.

Many dinosaur bones, such as this skull, had holes in them to help reduce the weight.

If two Tyrannosaurus wanted the same prey, they would probably have balanced their enormous bodies ready for attack and leaped forward with their mouths open. They used their strong tails to balance the weight of their bodies and strike their enemy. Tyrannosaurus ate large quantities of meat, which it swallowed whole; it could eat up to 26 pounds (12 kg) of meat in one bite. Tyrannosaurus also had very short arms; perhaps the animal used them to help push itself up from the ground.

Holding its prey firmly beneath its foot, one Tyrannosaurus roars a warning to another.

PREHISTORIC GIANTS

Extra-large eggs?

Some dinosaurs were enormous, and some were very small. Plant-eating dinosaurs had plenty of available food that enabled them to gain weight. Meat-eating dinosaurs had to increase their own size in order to hunt successfully. So, were dinosaur eggs enormous, too? Not as big as you might think. If they had been very big, the dinosaur babies would not have been able to break the thick shells. Just a few dinosaur eggs have been found. Some are only as big as a sparrow's egg; the largest measure about the size of a football.

Triceratops babies broke free of their eggs 70 million years ago.

One of the largest known dinosaurs was Brachiosaurus, which was as tall as a four-story building. One of the smallest was Compsognathus.

BRACHIOSAURUS

TYRANNOSAURUS

DEINONYCHUS

COMPSOGNATHUS

that there were duck-billed dinosaurs?

Duck-billed dinosaurs were unknown until the remains of an animal with a wide, flat mouth without teeth were discovered. This dinosaur was called Anatosaurus. Its wide mouth enabled it to collect huge quantities of plants. And, although it had no teeth at the front of its mouth, it did have them at the back of its jaws. Anatosaurus had hands like paddles, but did not live in the water. It probably escaped from predators by hiding in areas with shallow water.

Greedy Barosaurus

Barosaurus, or "heavy lizard," was an herbivore that ate from treetops 145 million years ago. It measured up to 90 feet (27 m) long; its neck alone could measure 33 feet (10 m). The vertebrae that formed its neck each measured almost 3.3 feet (1 m), but they were hollow so it could lift its head easily. Four giant, columnlike legs supported its 66-ton (60-metric ton) weight. Each foot had five toes. One toe on each front foot had a sharp, curved claw for self-defense.

Barosaurus could easily reach treetop leaves with its long, flexible neck.

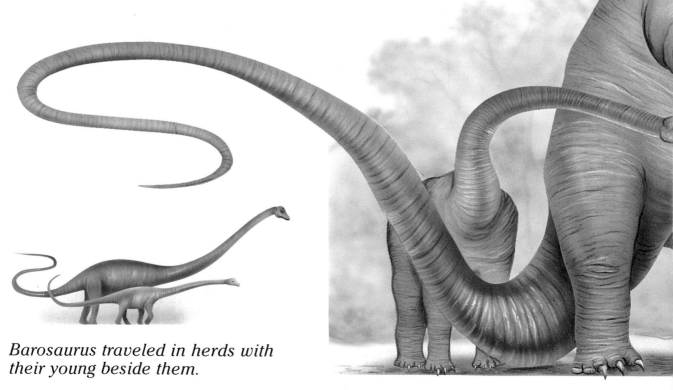

Barosaurus traveled in herds with their young beside them.

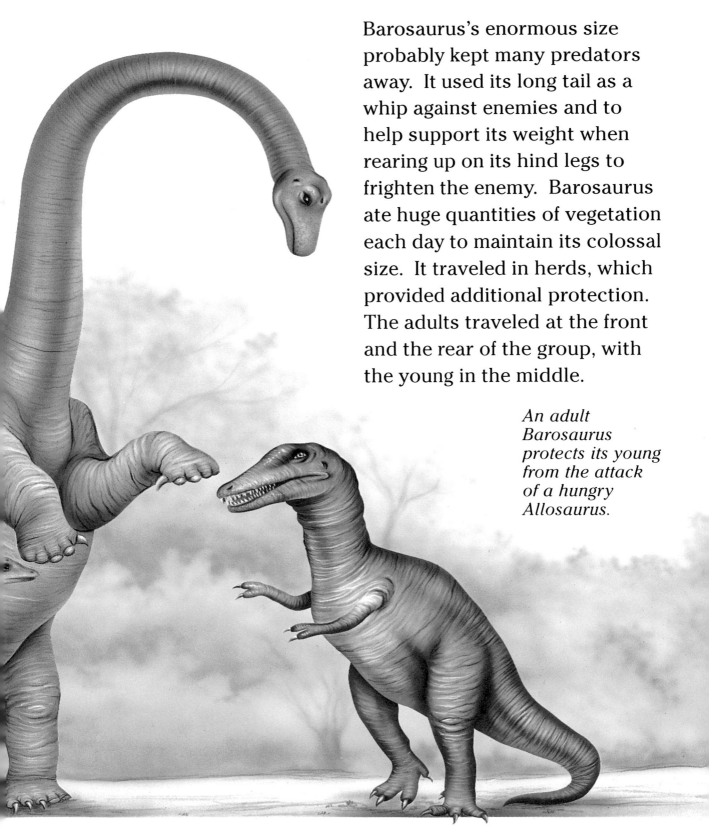

Barosaurus's enormous size probably kept many predators away. It used its long tail as a whip against enemies and to help support its weight when rearing up on its hind legs to frighten the enemy. Barosaurus ate huge quantities of vegetation each day to maintain its colossal size. It traveled in herds, which provided additional protection. The adults traveled at the front and the rear of the group, with the young in the middle.

An adult Barosaurus protects its young from the attack of a hungry Allosaurus.

DINOSAUR ANCESTORS

The first dinosaurs

Ancestors of the dinosaurs were reptiles that looked like today's crocodiles and lived more than 250 million years ago. According to paleontologists, the most probable dinosaur ancestor was Lagosuchus, a reptile 12 inches (30 cm) long that chased small prey by running on its long, slim back legs. The first great dinosaur was Plateosaurus. This plant-eating dinosaur could grow to more than 20 feet (6 m) long. It ate from treetops and, having no rivals of its own size, survived without difficulty. Other animals lived at the same time as the first dinosaurs: crocodiles; turtles such as Proganochelys, which could not draw either its head or feet into its shell; pterosaurs, or flying reptiles; and lizards, some of which were able to glide with the help of a special membrane.

Plateosaurus lived with other early reptiles and mammals in an environment very different from today's.

Today's mammals are descended from animals as terrifying as this sharp-toothed reptile.

Mammals descended from furry, reptilian beasts with long canine teeth. Scientists call them "dog's teeth" reptiles. These reptiles became extinct at about the same time as the dinosaurs appeared, but not before they evolved into the first mammals. These mammals were small, about the size of field mice, and they moved unnoticed in the dinosaur world.

Lagosuchus was a small reptile that ran swiftly on two feet. Scientists believe it was a forerunner of the dinosaurs.

that the dinosaurs did not become totally extinct?

Many scientists believe birds are direct descendants of dinosaurs. Some of the earliest birds, such as Archaeopteryx, may have evolved from small, agile dinosaurs that had a feather-like covering over their skin. Archaeopteryx could not fly, but it had wings that it used as a net to catch insects. Today's birds may be a result of adaptations in the dinosaurs. They have also developed the ability to fly. Birds may, therefore, be the only living representatives of the dinosaurs.

DINOSAUR BEHAVIOR

Looking for a mate

Male dinosaurs probably met in spectacular confrontations during mating season. In these situations, they fought to attract the females. For example, Triceratops's bony collar protected its neck and shoulders against predators, but it might also have changed color in a showy display to catch the attention of a female ready to mate. Rivalry among the males probably finished in a fight, as in the case of Stegoceras, a hard-headed, plant-eating dinosaur that lived in herds. The winner of the contest would become leader of the herd.

Although the skin color of dinosaurs is a mystery, some dinosaurs may have used skin color to attract mates.

Stegoceras's enormous "bump" protected it in fights during mating season, but it could also have broken some of its predators' bones.

Herbivore weaponry

Meat-eating dinosaurs had powerful, deadly weapons, but herbivores had them, too. Their weapons were used for defense rather than attack. Some plant-eaters defended themselves by sticking a sharp thumb claw or horn into an attacker. Other dinosaurs had a heavy club at the end of their tail. With a quick lash of the tail and a sharp blow from the club, they could even defeat Tyrannosaurus. Armor-plated dinosaurs defended themselves by lying still on the ground, hoping the enemy would be discouraged by their plates and spikes.

Predators had to be careful when attacking their victims, since they could be wounded and bleed to death.

Plant-eating dinosaurs could be aggressive when necessary.

Dinosaur mothers

In 1978, the remains of baby dinosaur skeletons and egg shells were found in a volcano-shaped nest. The baby dinosaurs' teeth were worn down, so scientists believe the parents brought them food in the nest. These dinosaurs were named Maiasaura, which means "good mother lizard." This Maiasaura nest was part of a group. Several mothers probably nested close together for protection. Other types of dinosaurs laid their eggs in holes instead of nests. Some took care of the young when they hatched; others left the young on their own.

The first fossilized dinosaur eggs ever found belonged to Protoceratops. This dinosaur laid several eggs in the same hole and covered them up using its back legs.

Some dinosaurs built nests, incubated the eggs, and fed their young.

APPENDIX TO

SECRETS OF THE ANIMAL WORLD

DINOSAURS
Monster Reptiles of a Bygone Era

DINOSAUR SECRETS

▼ **Eggs to eat.** Some dinosaurs had a very specific diet. Oviraptor, whose name means "egg thief," liked to eat other animals' eggs.

▼ **Dinosaur eggs.** Dinosaurs, like other reptiles, laid their eggs on land. The baby developed inside the egg with its tail curled around its body.

▼ **Noisy dinosaurs.** Parasaurolophus had a tubelike extension on its head. The tube may have been used to send an alarm or to frighten enemies.

Handy plate warmers. The bony plates on Stegosaurus's back protected it from predators. Some scientists believe the plates may also have been used to warm the dinosaurs in the early morning when the animals turned their plates to face the sun.

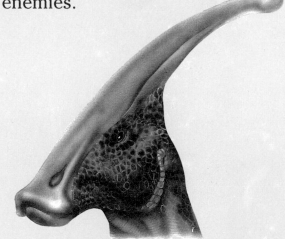

The dinosaurs' "grinder."
Piles of stones have been found beside the remains of herbivorous dinosaurs. Scientists believe the plant-eaters swallowed the stones to help them grind their food.

▶ **The bird imitator.**
Avimimus, or "bird imitator," ran across the plains of China and Mongolia 80 million years ago. Its front legs may have been covered in feathers.

Dinosaurs' ages. Scientists believe the dinosaurs probably lived for 60 to 70 years. Some may even have lived 100 years.

1. What did Tyrannosaurus use its tail for?
a) To help it get up.
b) To break down trees for food.
c) To keep its balance and strike its enemies.

2. What was the defense tactic of some armor-plated dinosaurs?
a) Lie still on the ground.
b) None; they were carnivores.
c) Escape to the marshes.

3. Which animals may be the direct descendants of the dinosaurs?
a) Crocodiles.
b) Birds.
c) Mammals.

4. In what way were dinosaurs different from lizards?
a) They did not have scales.
b) Their legs came straight down from their bodies.
c) They did not lay eggs.

5. What was special about Stegoceras?
a) A domed skull.
b) A terrible claw on its foot.
c) Spikes on the end of its tail.

6. The word *dinosaur* means:
a) Ancient reptile.
b) Ferocious mammal.
c) Terrible lizard.

The answers to DINOSAUR SECRETS questions are on page 32.

GLOSSARY

adaptation: the way an organism adjusts its behaviors and needs to survive in changing conditions.

aggressive: quick to start a fight or attack.

agile: nimble; able to move quickly and easily.

ancestors: previous generations.

ancient: very old; having existed for a long time.

bipeds: creatures that move about on two legs.

canine teeth: sharp, pointed teeth in front of an animal's mouth, used for tearing off pieces of meat or other tough food.

carnivore: a meat-eating animal.

colossal: huge in size; enormous.

competitor: an opponent; a person or group that opposes or is in conflict with another.

confrontations: aggressive encounters, such as fights or arguments.

continents: the large landmasses of Earth, which include Africa, Antarctica, Asia, Australia, Europe, North America and South America.

decay: a gradual breaking down.

defend: to protect oneself or one's possessions from danger.

descendants: living beings that have evolved or followed from particular ancestors.

droppings: solid body waste; excrement.

duck-billed: having a mouth or beak shaped like a present-day duck's bill. Hadrosaur, for example, was a duck-billed dinosaur.

environment: the surroundings in which plants, animals, and other organisms live.

evolve: to change shape or develop gradually over time.

extinct: no longer in existence.

ferocious: savage; brutal; fierce.

flexible: able to bend or move with ease.

forerunner: something or someone that has come before.

fossils: traces or remains of animals or plants from an earlier period of time that are often found in rock.

furrows: long, narrow grooves dug into the ground by a plow or some other tool.

glide: to move smoothly and quietly from one place to another.

herbivore: an animal that eats plants and other vegetable matter as its food source.

herds: large groups of animals that graze and live in groups in order to protect themselves from predators.

hollow: empty on the inside.

incubate: to keep warm and safe; most eggs need to be incubated between the time when they are laid and when they hatch.

insatiable: greedy; incapable of being satisfied.

lizards: scaly reptiles with slender bodies, long tails, and four legs that usually live in warm climates.

mammals: warm-blooded animals that have backbones. Female mammals produce milk to feed their young.

mate (v): to join together (animals) to produce young.

membrane: a thin, flexible layer of tissue in a plant or animal that lines or protects a certain part of its body.

pack: a group of similar or related animals that live and hunt together.

paleontologists: scientists who study life forms of past geologic periods; fossils are important to this kind of study.

predator: an animal that kills other animals for food.

prey: an animal that is hunted and killed for food by other animals.

pterosaurs: extinct flying reptiles that had featherless wings and an extended fourth finger.

rear (v): to rise up on the hind legs; to rise high in the air.

remains: what is left after something has died. Scientists obtain information about dinosaurs from fossil remains.

representative: a person or object that is typical of others of the same class.

reptiles: cold-blooded, egg-laying vertebrates that have lungs and dry, scaly skin, with claws on the toes. Snakes, lizards, and crocodiles are reptiles.

rivalry: a competition or contest between two or more parties.

species: animals or plants that are closely related and often similar in behavior and appearance. Members of the same species can breed together.

tyrant: a ruler that uses power cruelly or without justice.

vertebrae: any of the bones or cartilage segments forming the spinal column, or backbone.

vertebrates: animals that have backbones and internal skeletons, such as fish, reptiles, frogs, mammals, and birds.

ACTIVITIES

◆ If there is a college or university in your home town, find out whether the geology or biology departments have paleontologists or other scientists who study dinosaurs. Find out if you can interview one of these experts for your school paper. Ask the expert to speak to your class about working with dinosaur fossils.

◆ After studying several different kinds of dinosaurs, use clay or another medium to make models of them. Be sure to keep the body proportions accurate, since some dinosaurs were so much larger than others. For added fun, construct an environment for your dinosaurs based on what you have learned about them. Create a scene inside a cardboard box with crayons, paints, and paper.

◆ Make a list of all the different explanations scientists have suggested for what killed the dinosaurs. Which theory do you think is most likely, and why?

MORE BOOKS TO READ

Dinosaur Hunt! Rolf E. Johnson and Carol Ann Piggins (Gareth Stevens)
Dinosaurs and Prehistoric Life. (Running Press)
Dinosaurs: Unearthing the Secrets of Ancient Beasts. Don Nardo
    (Lucent Books)
Dinosaurs and Other Prehistoric Animals. Animals at a Glance series.
    (Gareth Stevens)
Modeling Dinosaurs. Draw, Model, and Paint series. Isidro Sanchez
    (Gareth Stevens)
The New Dinosaur Collection. 30 volumes. (Gareth Stevens)
The New Dinosaur Library. 4 volumes. (Gareth Stevens)
Over Sixty-five Million Years Ago: Before the Dinosaurs Died.
    Richard T. Moody (Macmillan)
Where to Find Dinosaurs Today. Daniel and Susan Cohen (Dutton)

VIDEOS

Dinosaur! An Amazing Look at the Prehistoric Giants.
    (Children's Video Library)
Dinosaur! Birth of a Legend: Tale of an Egg. (A&E Home Video)
The First Clue: Tale of a Tooth. (A&E Home Video)
The Infinite Voyage: The Great Dinosaur Hunt. (Vestron Video)

PLACES TO VISIT

Dinosaur Provincial Park
Route 873 (15 miles north
    of Brooks along the
    Red Deer River)
Patricia, Alberta T0J 2K0

**Royal Tyrrell Museum of
    Paleontology**
Dinosaur Trail
Drumheller, Alberta
T0J 0Y0

**The Field Museum of
    Natural History**
Roosevelt Road at Lake
    Shore Drive
Chicago, IL 60605

**The Smithsonian
    Institution**
1000 Jefferson Drive SW
Washington, D.C. 20560

Museum of Victoria
222 Exhibition Street
Melbourne, Victoria
Australia 3000

Otago Museum
419 Great King Street
Dunedin, New Zealand

INDEX

Answers to DINOSAUR SECRETS questions:
1. **c**
2. **a**
3. **b**
4. **b**
5. **a**
6. **c**